Grand Syllabus
Instructor Trainee
Program

Mors Kochanski

GRAND SYLLABUS

INSTRUCTOR TRAINEE PROGRAM

Survival, Wilderness Living Skills, Bushcraft

© Copyright 2015
ISBN: 978-1-894453-67-7
Published by Karamat Wilderness Ways

GRAND SYLLABUS

INSTRUCTOR TRAINEE PROGRAM

Survival, Wilderness Living Skills, Bushcraft

Suggested topics of interest to those who wish to become Survival Instructors, Wilderness Living Skills Instructors and Outdoor Educators.
Based on the life-long career of an Outdoor Educator

ENJOY YOUR WEALTH
DIE NOT IN GOOD HEALTH
LIFE MAY BE SHORT
DEATH IS SURE
WHEN IGNORANCE AND STUPIDITY ARE THE CAUSE
SOUND KNOWLEDGE IS THE CURE

MORS KOCHANSKI

CONTENTS

INSTRUCTOR COMPETENCY OUTLINE AND CHECKLIST

An "all inclusive" syllabus of topics once taught now and again by Mors Kochanski at the University level and in his Extended Summer and Winter Courses and the Survival Instructor Trainee Program (This program is no longer available).

This outline/checklist/syllabus attempts to list the topics one may consider to qualify as an **Instructor of Wilderness Living Skills and Survival** in the world. The time to master these topics likely exceeds 60 days of instruction backed by considerable practice over a number of years. A student works through the various levels of survival – Basic, Intermediate and Advanced as knowledge and skills develop. Ideally, students practice these wilderness skills at their own pace between sessions, with an hour of instruction backed by at least 10 hours of practice.

1. DEFINING SURVIVAL AND EXPOSURE

When exposed to any potentially lethal stresses commonly encountered in the wilderness, death is very likely if these stresses are not alleviated or eliminated soon enough. Survival knowledge is concerned with understanding these stresses so they can be dealt with effectively.

Always be aware of the tendency to overestimate one's abilities. Learn to recognize the warning signs of any developing danger.

EXPOSURE: There are certain possibly lethal stresses one encounters on becoming lost in the bush. It is important to recognize these stressors in time to be able to react to them before it is too late. These stressors should be anticipated and one should try to learn the best possible ways to deal with them. It is a little late to be learning how to swim when the boat is sinking out from under you in the middle of the lake and it is a little late to realize you should have brought along a life jacket.

To function properly (we are stating the obvious) the body tissues require fuel (oxygen and nutrition) recovery (rest and sleep), water and a constant temperature of 37° C.

Anyone lost in the wilderness will likely encounter the following stresses:

Disorientation plus
  Anxiety and **fear** equals
   Panic plus unusual **exertion** plus
    Hunger and the weakness that accompanies it leading
    to
     Fatigue which is made worse by
      Thirst which compromises energy and heat

delivery in the body resulting in
Chilling of the extremities with enough cold
discomfort to result in
Sleep deprivation which combined with
Pain, from some form of injury, all contributing
to
Exhaustion causing sleep from which you do
not wake
Within **40 hours** statistically, often on a nice
summer's day and
Death by "EXPOSURE" is the result.

Disorientation, anxiety fear and **panic** are predictable reactions experienced by anyone in unfamiliar environments. **Fear** is an unpleasant emotional state consisting of psycho-physiological response to real or imagined external threat or danger. Fear leads to increased tension, apprehension and decreased self-assurance. Become aware how you may be subjected to these stressors and learn how to avoid or control them. Learn how to relieve fear with breathing and other exercises. Fear that leads to **panic** may be controlled or eliminated if good training instills confidence in your ability to get by. Try to understand what tends to be the basis for your personal fears. Understanding the consequences of not eating, (**hunger**) becomes less terrifying if you realize it may take a month to die of starvation rather than day after tomorrow. Hunger indicates immediate body reserves are being depleted. You need fuel for the muscles and to maintain body temperature. If you continue not to eat you should know how to properly switch to the **fasting** mode. **Fatigue** (a general feeling of tiredness and decreased efficiency) is the body's way of warning you to slow down, rest and sleep. The circulatory system of the muscles becomes clogged with metabolic waste products. Rest provides the body with the opportunity to eliminate these by-products if you drink enough water. **Thirst**, is a sign of the dehydration that compromises your strength, your ability to think and the transfer of body warmth to the extremities, which emphasizes the importance of drinking enough water. Training would make you realize how serious cold stress or **chilling** can be and how it is countered by insulation in clothing and sleeping gear and the proper use of shelter and fire. The need for **sleep** must be addressed because it is inevitable and as cold keeps you awake until exhaustion forces you to succumb to it, perhaps becoming the final sleep from which you do not awaken. **Pain** indicates that something is wrong and it should usually be attended to before moving any further or it may intensify to the point where further movement becomes impossible. **Exhaustion** can be controlled to reduce its serious nature. Fatigue, pain and body reserve indicators may be ignored until the body shuts down so drastically you become unconscious. For a given individual there is a time limit to what can be endured before death. The ultimate objective of this syllabus is to help develop your awareness and capability in dealing with these and many of the other stressors.

2. THE TOOLS OF SURVIVAL AND THE TOOLS OF SURVIVAL TRAINING

The more you know, the less you carry. The less you know the more you carry. Pin down the essential knowledge of 'modern' survival techniques and back it up with some practice. Stack the deck in your favor with a well-chosen kit. With time you may reduce your dependence on most of your kit. There is no bush fairy that hits you across your head with a willow wand to magically transform you into a competent bushwhacker without a great deal of learning effort backed by considerable skill development. You do not learn to swim just by jumping in the water. Appreciate the importance of proper dress, sound fire skills, getting enough sleep and drinking enough water.

For survival the primarily focus is on the body's need for warmth, (heat does not come cheaply) sleep and water. Beyond this, survival is mostly a medical issue on understanding how the human mechanism is disrupted to compromise one's health and wellbeing.

The tools of survival:

1. Clothes
2. Fire
3. Knife
4. Personal First aid kit and appropriate first aid knowledge

The tools of survival training:

5. Navigation, map and compass or knowing how to get by without them
6. Sleeping bag 2/3 of importance and mat and bush bed 1/3
7. Pot of about 7 cups capacity
8. Shelter as derived totally or partially from nature and as a component of a kit
9. Signals
10. More tools - sawing and/or chopping tools, shovel etc.
11. Bindcraft - rope, paracord, jam knot, string, thread etc.
12. Pack frame and bag to contain gear

(I.) THE TOOLS OF SURVIVAL

3. CLOTHING

Clothing, the physiology behind the body's need for protection and the physics behind the clothing that provides it. You cannot walk on the moon without a space suit. *You cannot live comfortably in the bush without being appropriately dressed.* In the winter a properly dressed person may survive 4 days without a fire in deep snow at -40° C or F. Few things in a survival kit are more useful than a long, thick down coat. The key is to anticipate and control sweating by keeping comfortably cool or cold striving to keep skin temperature under 31°C. **Wet combined with wind is to be feared the most.**

- General principles and design features of clothing for dressing for summer/winter conditions.
- Differences between men and women in clothing design and reaction to cold and heat.
- Sanitary, insulation and environmental layers defined.
- Five insulation layers 4.5 cm max thickness with a tight-weave shirt used between any of the layers.
- A hood either doubles the effectiveness of a wind proof garment being the equivalent of a wool sweater but far more convenient to put on or take off. The same as a scarf or neck tube.
- The 'double stuffed' down coat.
- Just the careful combination of a set of clothes provides the benefit of a wool sweater more comfort.
- Three wool sweaters may keep you drier than normal rain gear.
- Wet weather clothing (including the canvas and wool blanket capes combined).
- Defining wet-cold and dry-cold.
- Wet and cold weather footwear – wear 3 pairs thick wool socks summer and winter.
- The importance of keeping clothes clean.
- Clothing repair (kits).
- Outstanding footwear-the Jungle boot and the Canadian military mukluk.

4. FIRE SKILLS AND THE TOOLS OF FIRELIGHTING

There are to major approaches to survival-the easy and the hard working.

The Easy: carry sufficient sleeping gear to avoid using a fire to keep warm while sleeping.

The Hard: surviving in your clothing, necessitates the gathering of fuel on a daily basis and maintaining a fire to stay warm when it is very cold.

After clothing, firecraft is the next most important skill. A proper warming fire without shelter or bed may allow you to survive for some time. The more urgent the need for fire the more challenging it is to make and maintain.

When to light a fire? When experiencing difficulty touching thumb to little finger of the same hand, light a fire immediately. Tend to use fire to stay warm rather than to thaw out.

What kind of fire? The parallel log fire is used 90% of the time; wall backed 5%; cross wood 5%. A cooking fire cooks clothing, a drying fire dries food. Drying fires are large so you can stand well back.

How big a warming fire? It is made up of logs of as large a diameter as possible about as long as you are tall, no shorter than nose to finger tip of the extended arm and the blaze big enough to force you to stay a step away. Warming fires are mostly moderated by the diameter of logs used.

Ignition: Lay down the three biggest logs you happen to have available, parallel to the wind and each other at four finger spacing. Build a good fire on these and lay on three more big logs for a fire that may last three or more hours. Can you light a fire after a three day rain in strong winds? Will your fire continue to burn during a heavy rain?

General fire skills:

- The science behind warming with infrared – the inverse cube law as a rule of thumb.
- The use of matches, large kitchen – level of challenge (Gr III elementary student), small-boxed (Gr VI) paper book matches (Gr IX) and split paper match (Gr XII).
- If you can light a fire in the rain and wind with a split paper match you are proving to yourself you are a very skilled fire lighter.
- Flint, carbon steel and tinder - something that catches a tiny spark and in turn lights kindling.
- Friction methods – bow drill, hand drill and fire plough.
- The use of the compact, indestructible, invincible (Zirconium) Fire Rod or metal match.
- Magnifying glass and parabolic reflector.
- Firearms/gun powder - not easy or dependable.
- Feather stick making with a sharp knife.
- Suitable fire sites with respect to fire hazard and ecological sensitivity.
- Extinguishing camp fires and developing a feel for forest fire hazard.
- The burning properties of firewood available in the coniferous forest.
- The burning properties of firewood available in the deciduous forest.
- The use of twigs:

  - The small handful.
  - The 'survival' twig bundle.
  - The hug size bundle.

- The twig torch.

- The use of natural *kindling – defined as a material that catches fire on the count of five.*
- ***The features of a well-constructed open fire.***
- The causes of smoky fires: wood too wet, too green, too big: fire too disorganized.
- Fires for **warmth** – the inverse cube law.
- The Finnish two log long burning fire (the King of warming fires).
- Fires for **cooking** – creating coals for cooking - suspension systems.
- Large fires for **drying** clothes and sleeping bags.
- Fires for producing more than the usual light.
- Fires for **incineration** – burning camp debris.
- Competitions as a means of testing for fire lighting competency.
- **Fire safety** in canvas tents, teepees and wigwams.
- Fire strategies without axe or saw – use of flip-flop winch to move heavy logs.
- How to avoid and treat burns and scalds.
- **Signal fires** (see (20) Signals Section)

  - minimal
  - standard
  - large or torch tree.

- **Smudges** against insects.
- Home built portable winter camping stoves.
- The science of combustion in stoves.
- Stovemanship – using (small) wood stoves safely and efficiently.
- Hazards, safe use and maintenance of backpacking stoves..
- The 4 Dog Stove Bush Cooker.
- Cooking and heating with stones.
- Using smoke to preserve fish and meat.
- An analysis of the various fire lays mentioned in the literature.

- The making of charcoal for blacksmithing.

5. THE KNIFE

A good survival knife is a pry-bar that works wood very well. **Can your 'survival' knife carve a netting needle and gauge within 10 minutes and yet be virtually unbreakable as with a pilot cutting his way out of a crashed plane?**

A knife is almost indispensible in survival. A blade 2 to 4 fingers long does 90% of knife work in survival and a blade 6 to 8 fingers 10%.

- An analysis of the features desired in a "survival" knife.
- A skilled knife user is aware of all the possible ways to injure one's self to avoid exacerbating any survival episode.
- Choosing an appropriate off-the-shelf knife – especially the scandi-ground MORA.
- How did the ancients get by without metal knives (as in "bare handed" survival).
- Sharpening knives to a shaving edge.
- The safe, efficient and powerful use of the knife including the baton.
- Cutting poles.
- Falling trees
- Loss proofing a knife
- Projects to develop the safe and skillful use of the knife:

  o The try stick
  o The netting needle and gauge
  o Eating/stirring spatulas
  o Some folk toys
  o Four curls (beginner) or more in the making of feather sticks
  o Carving faces
  o The Siberian bow trap for small game

     o   Making replacement sheaths for knives

6. PERSONAL FIRST AID KITS

Kit # 1 To fit a shirt pocket (primarily to deal with knife cuts in particular) consisting of the following items:

- 6 Curity Telfa Pads 10 X 7.5 cm
- 12 Elastoplast anchor (knuckle) dressings
- 1 tube Polysporin ointment (3.5 grams) ophthalmic – preferred – eye injury common
- 1 package (10) Steri-Strips 3m (butterfly closures)
- **1 signal mirror** (5 X7 cm) so that it is always on you and to remove objects from the eye.
- 1 good tweezers, sharp pointed and fine-tuned with a fold of 600 grit sand paper
- 2 Sewing needles, medium size, pre-threaded ready to use
- 3 meters or a small spool of dental floss
- 1 small compass
- 1 small metal match
- 1 whistle high tech or properly made from a strip of tin when needed

Kit # 2 In second shirt pocket providing the components to deal with an axe cut if one is used.

Kit # 3 Fanny-pack kit for dealing with chainsaw injuries where appropriate.

First aid kits for group use and extended expeditions.

7. DEALING WITH ACCIDENTS – BASIC FIRST AID AND MEDICAL KNOWLEDGE

There should be a focus on first aid for common injuries that do not necessarily need professional medical attention.

A great deal of survival is a matter of medicine. The best survival instructor should also be a MD and be married to an emergency-room nurse. There are various courses available in wilderness emergency medicine to augment what is suggested in this syllabus. In addition consider the following:

- The **prevention – mitigation – rehabilitation** approach to accidents.
- Staying healthy – maintaining a high **immune response.**
- Avoiding infectious diseases – **breaking the chain of contagion.**
- Inflammation, infection and the process of **wound healing.**
- Studying the art of avoiding **knife and axe cuts** specifically.
- Cleaning and closing wounds – dealing with **cuts up to 8 stitches.**
- Dealing with **simple fractures** for evacuation – improvising splints –dealing with sprains.
- Reducing dislocations.
- How to tape sprained ankles - dealing with sprains.
- How to monitor vital signs.
- How to give injections.
- How to recognize, avoid and treat (likely in anticipation of evacuation to a medical facility):

  - **Hypothermia** and frostbite.
  - Hyperthermia and **heat illnesses.**
  - **Dehydration** and water purity.

- Normal scalds and burns.
- Exposure to UV and snow blindness.
- Boils.
- Nosebleed.
- Shock.
- Artificial respiration.
- Foreign object in the eye.
- Simple fainting.
- Poisoning by mouth – food – plants - mushrooms.
- Heart attacks, strokes and vascular health.

- How to avoid and deal with **ticks** and biting spiders.
- How to avoid snakes and deal with snake bite.
- **Natural remedies**

(examples found in the Boreal Forest):

- Fir and black poplar balsam for burns, scalds and wounds.
- Plantain poultices for skin lesions.
- Labrador tea for burns, scalds and diarrhea.
- Willow inner bark for headaches.
- Fairy pelt lotion for skin rashes.
- Bearberry tea for fevers and bladder infections.
- The many uses of the panacea sweet flag (Rat root).

- Stretcher construction and use and the transportation of the injured.
- Crutch construction and use.
- Dental health and tooth emergencies.

8. MINIMUM PREPAREDNESS – CLOTHING, MATCHES, KNIFE AND FIRST AID KIT

Emphasis on the minimum gear one strives to carry for the possibility of having to survive.

Causes of (wilderness) mishaps:

1. Carelessness and blunders.
2. Overestimation of physical stamina.
3. Over estimation of one's technical ability.
4. Overconfidence.
5. Misinformation.
6. Inadequate knowledge and experience.
7. The failure of attitude.
8. The failure of unpreparedness.

Preparedness entails carrying the right equipment and rations and foreseeing dangerous situations in time. ***You are often embroiled in some dangerous event likely because of something you didn't know about and then it's called an "accident".*** Think and study the situation before you dive into it.

You should be self-sufficient in sustenance, keeping warm, navigating and recognizing the hazards that may entrap you. Readiness involves advanced planning and preparation and appreciating the importance of mental and physical fitness and training.

(II.) THE TOOLS OF SURVIVAL TRAINING

9. NAVIGATION

A leader must never get lost as this is a serious professional responsibility. **There is no excuse for becoming lost as a leader. Know your position at all times. Your location, surroundings, future route, changing conditions, and changes of plans must be constantly communicated to your party.**

- Basic compass use (see also (19.) On The Move Summer and Winter).
- The various compass types .
- Natural direction indicators.
- Pacing to keep track of distance – 1000 paces, 2000 steps per mile; 625 paces per kilometer..
- The Swedish pole-compass.
- The Owendoff (crude) shadow-pole method of determining a direction.
- The use of a watch as a compass.
- Some stars useful in navigation.
- Reacting to personal disorientation - use blazing or wads of moss or vegetation to mark trail.
- Travel and reading the terrain, picking safe routes and appraising difficulties in terrain.
- The zigzag method of using natural avenues through forest stands on a given bearing.
- The use maps currently available.
- Interpreting access topographic maps and their legends.
- Aerial photographs.
- Basic Global Positioning Technology (GPS).
- Some pointers on sketching your own maps.

10. THE SLEEPING BAG, MAT AND BED

About a third of one's existence is devoted to sleep. How long can you go without sleep before becoming your own worst enemy? The longer you are awake the more you think and act as if drunk. When lost your prime concern is not your next meal but rather how you are to get the sleep when you need it. The inexperienced camper usually brings too much food and too little sleeping gear. You may sleep hungry and warm but not well fed and cold.

The quality of any survival instruction may be evaluated by how well one achieves adequate sleep in spite of the severity of prevailing conditions.

- Defining adequate sleep – a minimum of two hours rapid eye movement sleep every twenty-four.
- The need for restful sleep.
- The relevance of sleeping gear in survival kits.
- How to choose a suitable sleeping bag.
- The relationships of sleeping bags, mats, beds, fire and clothes.
- Supplementing an inadequate bag.
- The use of open cell and closed cell mattresses.
- Beds made of natural materials, minimal, standard and deluxe.
- Mat looms and mats made of braids or rope pinned together with dags.
- The bed as a form of stretcher.
- Bag maintenance, drying out and laundry.
- Ploys in getting by without a sleeping bag.
- The survival scarf comforter.
- The double-stuffed down jacket.

11. WATER REQUIREMENTS

The POT of at about 7 cups capacity useful for boiling, measuring and carrying water.

To survive one must get enough sleep and drink enough water.

The sense of thirst is a poor indicator of dehydration. Drinking enough water as prevention of the rapid **onset of fatigue, frostbite and hypothermia.** The need for water is preceded only by that for oxygen. It is the medium for all body fluids involving blood, lymph, digestive juices, urine and perspiration. It participates in osmotic pressure relationships, acid-base balances, movements of nutrients into cells and the elimination of metabolic wastes. **Dehydration** is dependent on low humidity, winds, direct and reflected sunlight, compromised thirst reduced water consumption or loss and specific hormonal changes.

Dehydration has a negative effect on muscular exertion, mental activity, cold tolerance and the transfer of metabolic warmth from the body core to the extremities making hypothermia and frostbite worse. An adult is 55 to 65 % water. A loss of 10% results in illness, 20% the possibility of death.

- The physiology of thirst.
- Thirst being an inadequate means to monitor dehydration.
- Stages of dehydration – 1. Orange colored urine. 2. Persistent headache. 3. Nausea on eating.
- Irritability, headache, poor judgment and degraded cold tolerance usually occur in water deficit.
- The importance of drinking enough water, especially in winter.
- Pass a minimum of a liter daily regardless of intake *with some color* to the urine.
- During fasting drink 7 cups of hot water for breakfast.
- Water, fasting and dealing with hunger pangs.
- Sources of water in the wilderness.
- Looking for water in scarce and (desert) situations.

- Melting snow for drinking water.
- Purifying water – by boiling, clear polyethylene bottles, stills, filtration and chemicals –pros & cons.
- The simple Australian pipe distiller.
- The implications of drinking hot (deoxygenated), tepid and cold water.
- "Activated" water.
- 'Eating' snow.
- Oral rehydration therapy – grape Tang crystals.
- Kit components for carrying, storing or purifying water.
- Canteens.
- Water unavailable – drinking little on day one to put the kidneys into conservation mode.
- Water-borne diseases especially giardiasis.

12. SHELTER IS THE CLOTHING OF THE GROUP
CLOTHING IS THE SHELTER OF THE INDIVIDUAL

All the science an architect uses to design a good house (such as thermal mass, absorption, re-emission, reflection, emissivity, infrared etc.) no less applies to building any wilderness shelter. *Open lean-to construction and use is very poorly rendered in current survival literature.*

- Choosing a campsite for the greatest benefit (for open fronted shelters).
- The five distinct components of an open lean-to with a fire in front.
- Basic shelters of natural materials.
- Kit component shelters:

    o the open lean-to.
    o greenhouse type emergency shelter.
    o the "super" shelter that imitates the features of an igloo.

- The wigwam and teepee used with internal and external open fires.
- Mosquito-proof shelters.
- The winter 'thermal' shelter – pay attention to the science.
- The snow houses made of snow blocks wind or snowshoe packed .
- The snow shelters made of loose snow.
- Using stoves in shelters.
- Lighting inside shelters.
- Choice of shelter site for optimal insulation - the cosine law.
- Unsafe campsite – river and sand or gravel bar – falling rock – falling trees and limbs – plants - insects and animal pathways.

13. THE AXE AND HATCHET

If allowed only one tool, the axe may be a good choice. **To become a skilled and safe axe user may require at least a week of eight-hour days of training and practice to avoid direct cuts to the body and injury from the falling tree itself.** Women are better learners tending to focus on accuracy while men tend to think power works better.

Student: "Can you teach me how to survive without an axe?
Instructor: "Do you know how to use an axe?"
Student: "No, that's why I wish to learn how to survive without one!"
Instructor: "How can anyone teach you how to survive without an axe when you don't know how to use one?"

There is no short cut to learning how to cope here. In Boreal survival wood fuel and shelter materials are usually plentiful but sometimes not readily accessible without tools.

- The bigger the axe the safer and the more effective in getting any work done but is awkward to carry.
- A hatchet and a big saw are a passable combination.
- The general features of a good axe.
- The full sized axe.
- The ¾ or boy's axe.
- The ½ or carpenter's axe.
- The camper's hatchet.
- Choosing an appropriate axe with survival in mind.
- Axe sharpening.
- The safe and efficient use of axes.
- Being one axe handle ahead.
- Replacing axe handles in the shop and in the field.
- Axe sheaths.
- The art of splitting firewood.
- Splitting long logs with wedges.

14. THE SAWS

The saw is many times safer than an axe, being a better initial choice for the learner. Wedges can be used in falling with a saw, not possible with an axe alone. Unlike the axe it can be used after dark to section trees. All falling is best done in daylight. **The axe is the more versatile tool.** Learning to use a saw is like learning to use snowshoeing while the axe is like learning cross country skiing. **The best complementary combination is a big enough axe and a big enough saw.**

- Choosing an appropriate saw in context with various survival objectives –wood - snow.
- A saw blade encased in a waist belt holding up your pants is an excellent survival kit component.
- The safe use of the saw.
- The use of wedges in felling.

- Some shortcomings of saws.
- Sharpening and setting saw teeth.
- Constructing saw frames when only the blade is carried in a pot or waist belt .
- The small folding (crafting) saw.
- An excellent folding buck saw.
- The Swedish board saw for cutting wood and snow blocks for igloo building.
- Wire saws.

15. SOME USEFUL TOOLS FOR THE REMOTE OUTBACK

With a handful of the metal bits of some well-chosen tools one may build almost anything needed in primitive living.

- The awls, round, square or triangular.
- The spoke shave.
- The spoon gouge.
- The ½ inch wood chisel.
- The small metal cutting chisel.
- The Eclipse hacksaw.
- The crooked knife.
- The gimlet.
- Bow drill wood boring bits.

16. BINDCRAFT- KNOTS, ROPE WORK AND CORDAGE

Bindcraft is a significant bottleneck in survival and bushcraft. Almost every primitive artifact or structure is lashed together. Any spare space in a survival kit should be filled with 550-200-7 parachute shroud line (550 pound test, 200 safe working load, 7 the number of strands).

- Some local cordage materials, grass, nettle, dog bane and cattail.
- Bind craft with locally available materials.
- The types of cordage useful to pack in survival kits.
- The most useful bush knots, **especially the JAM knot** - the most useful knot in creation.
- Methods of lashing with cordage other than para cord.
- Methods of lashing with relatively weak natural materials.
- Various rope spinning devices.

17. MOVING HEAVY OBJECTS WITH ROPE AND POLES

Rope and poles can provide significant mechanical advantages.

- Don't lift what you can drag or roll.
- Disassemble where possible to reduce weight.
- Big weights may be moved if done slowly enough.
- The Spanish, Finnish and flip-flop windlasses.

18. SNOWCRAFT

Snow is a marvelous resource if one is familiar with its useful properties.

- Snow formations – snow and wind - drifts, snowcrete, Snow fences.
- Effect of snow cover on winter weather and climate.
- The escalation of characteristics with lowering temperature especially the abrasive nature of snow and ice. At 60 below Celsius ice is as abrasive as gravel.
- Definition of wet cold and dry cold.
- Snow loads on man- made structures.
- Snow loads on ice – Snow – ice interactions.
- Snow shelters.

- Snow – reflectivity –insulation – conductivity.
- Oxygen permeability of snow in snow shelters.
- Melting snow for potable water – energy implications.
- Eating' snow.
- Snow shelters.
- Skis and snowshoes.
- Snow – ground interactions.
- Avalanches.
- Travel hazard on snow covered rivers and lakes.
- Snow and animal life.

19. ON THE MOVE (WITH AND WITHOUT A LOAD) SUMMER AND WINTER

The art and science of moving a burden is indispensible in wilderness living skills.

- Walking – rhythm – balance – length of stride – knee bend – hip action – speed – distances –hills.
- Optimal speed 4 km/hour (3 ½ mph for men, 2 ½ mph for women) at 330 Calories per hour.
- For 5 to 6 mph (beyond 160 paces per minute) a slow run is better than a fast walk.
- Running is optimal at 220 paces per minute.
- At 70 rpm cycling is twice as economical as walking.
- A good eight hours travel:

  o Walking on road – 25 miles.
  o Walking in woods – 10 miles.
  o Horse on country road – 35 miles.
  o Canoe on lake – 25 miles.
  o Canoe downstream - 30 miles depending on current.
  o Canoe upstream – 20 miles depending on current.

- The Roycraft pack frame, construction and use.
- Load limits and the physiology of backpacking.
- Various methods of slinging a load.

- The bag to contain one's gear and its use for other purposes.
- The travois.
- Walking staffs as a significant energy saver.
- General travel hints.
- Route finding.
- The advantages and hazards of following rivers summer and winter.
- Zigzag navigation by the use of natural corridors.
- Hazards relevant to travel in various terrain including high elevations.
- Snowshoes, skis, sleds and toboggans.
- Emergency snowshoe construction.
- The construction and use of emergency toboggans.
- The hazards of travelling on the ice, lakes and rivers.
- ***River crossing in summer – the biggest killer of all wilderness hazards combined.***
- Safe travel on river and lake in summer – boat - canoe.
- The hazards of traveling on the ice, lakes and rivers ice thickness, moving and static loads.
- Horsemanship - saddle, pack, cart and wagon.
- Breaking through the ice with a horse.
- The dog – pack and sled.
- Boatmanship - canoe – boat – coracle and raft.
- The mountain bicycle.
- The snowmobile.
- The ATV.
- The 4 by 4.
- Aircraft travel as a passenger hazard.
- An introduction to the hazards of flying.

20. SIGNALS, SIGNS, TRAIL MARKERS AND BLAZING

Signaling your distress requires the knowledge of the conventions understood by rescuers.

- The objectives in signaling.
- The signal mirror – 16 km visibility.
- The signal fire and its variants – very poorly covered in the current literature.
- The ground to air code.
- Sound signals.
- Signal flares.
- Body signals,
- Dye to discolor snow (potassium permanganate and calcium chloride).
- United Nations Blue as the most visible color.

21. RADIO COMMUNICATIONS

Be familiar with the local means of communication used in your region.

22. SANITATION IN THE BUSH CAMP

Personal cleanliness is important when sharing a camp with others. Certain poor habits can result in preventable gastro-intestinal distress.

- Personal hygiene – bathing - oral.
- The construction of the steam bath.
- Washing eating and cooking utensils – proper waste water disposal.
- Laundry methods.
- Camp manners in general and in connection with hygiene.
- The construction and maintenance of latrines.
- Group latrines.
- Dispersed individual usage.
- Digging with or without a shovel - the chisel pole.
- Getting by without toilet paper.
- Conduct in sensitive ecological areas.
- Garbage disposal - what to do about empty cans.

- Burnable garbage – when and how to burn - avoid burning plastics.
- Disposing of leftover food.

23. SUMMER OUTDOOR HAZARDS

- Bears
- Cougars
- Wolverine
- Wolves
- Moose
- Snakes
- Rodents and the Hantavirus
- Other fearsome animals
- Forest fire
- Insects – mosquitoes - blackflies - wasps
- Racoons
- Other

24. WINTER OUTDOOR HAZARDS

- Relevant to the winter cold
- Relevant to tool use
- Relevant to confined living, - carbon monoxide - shelter conflagration.
- Loosing equipment in the snow.

25. THE HAZARDOUS NATURE OF THE MOUNTAINS

Everything at high altitude works against one's survival in the event of an emergency.

Above tree line: Poor fuel sources – few plants – few identifiable features – sudden and violent weather changes – scant shelter from the wind –snow and glaciers – rarified oxygen – crevices and cavities, water flow under the snow, avalanches and falling rock.

Ultraviolet radiation (UV): At high elevations there is less filtering of UV rays. Ice and snow may reflect 75% of UV rays. UV on overcast days can cause severe sunburn and snow blindness.

Weather: The temperature drops a few degrees with every 30 meters of ascension. Winds at higher elevations usually blow more strongly. The decreased visibility in heavy rain, thick fog and clouds requires continuous reference to your compass. Conditions contribute to a loss of a sense of passage of time so you are caught out on the mountain by darkness.

Lightening: Exposed ridges and summits are frequently struck.

Physiological stresses: The higher the elevation, the harder lungs, circulatory system and the heart have to work. Over two weeks may be needed to acclimatize to high elevations.

Oxygen: At 18,000 feet you are at half normal value of atmospheric oxygen that may cause brain oxygen starvation. Digestion robs oxygen from muscles and brain and exertion robs oxygen from digestive system and brain.

The discomforts of altitude: Headache, shortness of breath, insomnia and nausea are common.

Slippery slopes: Snow, frosty – wet – dry – grass, how do you stop sliding down the slope?

Exceeding altitude limit: Un-acclimatized person acts intoxicated (higher than14,000 ft.)

Gaining altitude too quickly, going too high: Acute mountain sickness – high altitude pulmonary edema – and high altitude cerebral edema: with altitude there are lower oxygen levels and higher carbon dioxide levels in the blood to cause blood vessels to expand and the fluids in the blood tending to leak out to cause edema in lungs and brain – **Descend immediately!**

26. THE WEATHER

Be prepared for the worst weather possible. <u>Wet combined with wind are to be feared the most.</u>

- Keep weather in mind when making decisions while surviving.
- Obtaining weather information by radio or telephone.
- Forecasting for fair weather, rain, snow and frost within one's own horizons.
- Lightning hazard.
- Hurricane hazard.
- Tornado hazard.
- Violent wind hazard.
- Flooding hazard.

27. SURVIVAL KIT DESIGN AND USE

A backpacker carries an ideal comprehensive survival kit weighing 70 pounds. A survival kit should be less than 10% of that, yet achieve as much by incorporating natural materials A kit should mostly address two major points: (1) Does it aid you in sleeping better and (2) Help in meeting your water needs? Field test any kit on which your life and safety may depend.

- Emphasis on kits useful in the summer and winter.
- Analysis of some useful kit components.
- Space age indispensables – metal match – nylon parachute shroud line – mylar and poly film.
- Examination of some conventional, perhaps useless kit components commonly sold or mentioned in the literature.
- The Coleman lantern as a survival tool in vehicle travel.

28. THE MENTAL-PHYSICAL ASPECTS OF SURVIVAL

Your mind can play an important role in your survival. The stresses generated by an uncontrolled mind may quickly result in death. Psychological turmoil is at its greatest in the first three days of a survival incident. Rest in a safe place and wait three days before engaging in any serious, physically-demanding exertion and to acclimatize to your given situation. Allow your memory time to recall a surprising amount of useful information. With nothing to eat rest long enough for the fasting state to develop (at least 3 days). (See Section 37-Food Quest)

- How one manages with the physical discomforts and stresses may have a more profound effect on one's mental attitude rather than the actual physical imposition.
- Adapt to your surroundings.
- Think out all pros and cons before you act.
- Imagined fears of the unknowns should be replaced by real – keep your imagination under control.
- Panic – The sudden, irrational reaction to a perceived threat must be studied to acquire the mental resources to control it.
- Depression, hopelessness and helplessness are to be expected in survival episode.
- Type A personalities fair badly.

- Peace of mind – confidence – speculation on how these may be achieved.
- Positive and negative mind sets.
- Exercises to reduce stress such as breathing and meditation.
- Psychological preparation – you are warmer if you are psychologically prepared for cold.
- Risk management.
- Acute fatigue: - accumulation of metabolite by products – poor fitting clothes – Overloading (carrying excessive weight) – working in spells – using different muscles – the consequences of being anemic and other deficiencies – dehydration – food type and lack thereof.
- Chronic fatigue – the psychology involved – overwork.
- The drive to survive may diminish with time.

29. THE NEEDS OF WIVES, MOTHERS AND CHILDREN UNDER SURVIVAL DURESS

- Clothing: Weaving cloth – tanning hides for clothing – looms.
- Cooking.
- Children – cradle boards – (disposable) diapers.
- Sanitary napkins.
- Laundry.
- Beds and bedding.

30. THE WILD PLANTS FOUND IN SUMMER SAID TO BE EDIBLE, USEFUL, MEDICINAL, MAGICAL AND POISONOUS

Initially, one should master a minimum of 250 plants and after that every plant found nearby.

- The flowering plants
- The common trees
- The shrubs

- The lichens
- The ferns
- Sphagnum moss
- Mushrooms

31. THE WILD PLANTS FOUND IN WINTER

Although plant use is quite restricted in the winter there are still some valuable plants to know.

- Dendrology (the study of trees)
- The shrubs
- The lichens
- Sphagnum moss and other mosses
- Other

32. THE FAUNA

Know enough of the natural history of the animals in your environment to avoid them when they are hungry and to catch them when you are hungry. The natural history of any fearsome animal requires considerable study. A few pages of do's and don'ts do not provide enough useful information to adequately manage any life threatening encounters with them.

- Where appropriate the traps deadfalls and snares for these animals.
- Discussion of the natural history of the following animals in so far as related to survival:

  - moose, deer and elk, pronghorn, bighorn sheep, and mountain goat
  - varying hares and rabbits
  - ruffed grouse
  - voles
  - coyotes
  - gray jay, chickadee and nuthatch

- o various woodpeckers
- o porcupines
- o bears
- o grizzlies
- o wolverines
- o wolves
- o cougars
- o red squirrels

- Uses of animal materials: 1. Sinew 2. Meat 3. Fat 4. Gut 5. Bladder 6. Bone 7. Antler 8. Hair 9. Vitreous humor 10. Feathers 11. Quills 12. Glue

33. WEAPONS

The modern survivalist must realize the difficulties of making functional weapons under survival conditions. Acquire the basic knowledge with respect to the following:

- Rifle
- Shotgun
- Handgun
- Bow and arrow
- Crossbow
- Blowgun
- Boomerang / Rabbitstick
- Atlatl
- Spear
- Fish spear
- Sling
- Gun powder

34. TRAPS, DEADFALLS AND SNARES

Compared to hunting traps can provide game with minimal energy expenditure, working while you are engaged with other tasks when you are asleep. Traps are more readily constructed than weapons. The construction of these devices may depend on the tools available. The construction of the appropriate traps, deadfalls and snares pertaining to the animals in Section 32. THE FAUNA.

35. THE ART OF FISHING

Fish as sustenance in survival - the nutritional value of fish. Hooks and fish line occupy little space and weight in a comprehensive kit. Fishing is simpler and easier than hunting.

- In the choice of fly lures (dry, wet and nymph) the size of fly and its shade from light to dark that has a movement that is attractive to fish is key.
- The Grey Nun may catch more different kinds of fish than any other lure. Have a good selection of sizes, shapes and shades rather than individual patterns. For bigger northern fish a collection of different spoons is all you need.
- Fish hooks – lures: **The Upperman bucktail jig** may take over a 100 species of fish. It was the only lure packed in the WWII U. S. Navy survival kits. A No. 10 forged hook and a chamois streamer cut in the shape of a minnow less than an inch long. Let sink deep and retrieve in jerks.
- Fish traps.
- Fish nets.
- Fish spears.
- Spool fishing vs. long pole fishing.
- Constructing fish nets and using them.

36. THE INSECTS

There are rare occasions when insects are a significant source of food. The annoyance of biting insects is a serious aspect of living in any remote wilderness.

- Annoying insects of the North
- Insects as vectors in disease
- The edible insects
- The useful insects

37. THE FOOD QUEST

In modern basic survival living off the land is deferred until the important skills of fire, bed and shelter are mastered. When expectation of rescue is considered remote, intermediate survival is applicable and living off the land has its place. In advanced (as in preparing for some Apocalypse) skillful living off the land is very relevant.

- Fasting and conduct when unable to live off the land.
- Differentiating between food deprivation, fasting and starvation.
- When to live off the land and when to fast.
- Strategies in living off the land - animals and plants as food.
- The edible plants.
- The edible mushrooms.
- The edible lichens.
- Wilderness gardening.
- Rabbit starvation.
- Food preservation – dehydrating, smoking, canning, salting, freezing, storage.

38. PROVISIONING GROUPS (FOR STUDENTS ON COURSES)

- Basic provisioning
- Provisioning for (large) groups
- Designing recipes
- The value of appropriate condiments
- The two meal day

39. PROVIDING LIGHT by PRIMATIVE METHODS

- Candles and candle lanterns
- Primitive lamps using oil or grease
- Resin saturated splints
- The Eskimo kudlik
- Resin on trees
- Lighting the tip of an almond
- The twig torch
- The Finnish torch
- The conical wood stacked fire for light

40. OUTDOOR COOKING

- The appropriate fire types for group cooking.
- The various suspension systems.
- The choice of cooking and eating utensils for expeditions.
- Cooking in pits.
- Bear avoidance cooking.
- Cook away from camp (on the fly).
- Cooking food odors and sleeping gear.
- Packaging smelly foods.
- Avoiding smelly foods.
- Burning food or garbage as a means of disposal attracts unwanted animals.

41. CACHING TECHNIQUES

The cache is prone to various types of damage from dampness, mildew and rodents:

- Airtight containers highly desirable
- Hiding caches
- Protection from rodents
- Protection from bears and wolverines

- Caching in springs and ant hills to protect canned goods from freezing
- The hazard of caching near rivers
- The tree cache (involving a ladder)

42. PRIMATIVE TOOLS AND PROCESSES

The basic processes, using primitive tools:

- To cut - saw - chop - scrape – split - abrade - grind – polish - crush - pound- peck - dig holes
- Avoiding overloading a tool to the point of destruction.

43. WHAT CAN BE CONSTRUCTED MOSTLY WITH STRAIGHT STICKS, POLES AND CORD

These projects are mostly isolated out of previously mentioned headings.

- Walking staff, canes, crooks.
- Owendorf shadow direction determination.
- Sundial.
- Point staff at sun to observe nature of shadow movement and its application in determining direction.
- Arrow, atlatl dart, fish spear and lance.
- Tent poles and pegs - building anchors with pegs.
- Pot suspensions for cooking.
- Bridges.
- Stretchers and beds.
- Sail masts and spars.
- Teepee poles and tripods.
- Roycraft pack frame and ski shoes.
- Digging pole.
- Winches – Spanish, Finnish and flip flop.
- Fire tongs.

- Mat looms.

44. NATURAL CRAFTING

- Weaving and doll making out of cattail
- Basket weaving with willow
- Flutes and whistles
- Basket weaving out of spruce splints
- Composite baskets
- Decoys of tamarack and other twigs
- Various folk toys
- The bull roarer
- Games and puzzles
- Bark baskets and buckets.

45. PRIMATIVE BLACKSMITHING AND CASTING

- Making forges.
- Making charcoal.
- Making simple tools - awls, chisels, drill bits, arrowheads, flint and steel strikers.
- Making crucibles and casting molds out of sandstone.

46. PERSONAL AND HOME SECURITY CONSIDERATIONS

- Various crisis situations
- Methods of self defense
- Dealing with marauders
- Fortifications

47. DURING EXTENDED COURSE TRAINING THE STUDENT MAY HAVE THE OPPORTUNTIY TO CONSTRUCT OR ASSEMBLE THE FOLLOWING WHERE

AVAILABILITY OF MATERIALS AND TIME PERMITS

1. A survival camp to include: a lean to, a bough bed, a wall backed fire, and a signal fire.
2. A survival kit component movable super shelter.
3. If adequate snow is available, the classic form of snow shelter – quinzee and igloo.
4. A small personal enclosed shelter heated by a primitive stove.
5. A group shelter heated by an open fire.
6. A buck saw.
7. A pair of Roycraft emergency ski-shoes.
8. A Roycraft pack frame.
9. A general purpose polyethylene rope made with a rope maker of some sort.
10. Rope, cordage or string that may be made of sedge, hairy wild rye grass, wolf willow bark, Bebb's willow bark, dog bane, stinging nettle or cattail.
11. A wire snare for varying hare rabbit and squirrel.
12. A primitive bow and arrow for hunting squirrel .
13. A lifting pole string snare for hare.
14. A netting needle and gauge and a few square feet of net.
15. A fire by friction bow and drill set.
16. A flint and steel set.
17. Numerous feather sticks for fire lighting.
18. A twig torch .
19. A primitive lamp (kudlik) using fat as fuel.
20. A simple willow basket.
21. A composite basket.
22. A cattail doll.
23. A carving made out of black poplar bark..
24. A tin whistle.
25. Whistles and flutes made of cow parsnip or plastic water pipe.
26. A bull roarer.
27. A birch bark knife sheath.
28. A walking staff.
29. Carved eating spatulas and spoons.

30. Sharpening boards.
31. A collection of the plants found during courses.
32. A try stick to demonstrate knife competency.
33. Using coals, burn out a wooden spoon, bowl or ladle.
34. A Siberian bow trap for ermine.
35. A beaver deadfall trap.
36. A steam bath.

Hints to Competent Instruction

HINTS TO LEADER - INSTRUCTORS

Pointers on being a competent leader - instructor and the survival training process

(1)A competent leader - instructor errs on the side of caution, when the welfare of others is assumed but at the same time is not timid when faced with a situation requiring bold action.

The leader – instructor prepares adequately for emergencies when embarking on any ambitious enterprise where there is any possibility of injury or fatality.

(2)Knowing how to cope with survival problems under the most challenging conditions rates high.

(3)One should be sensitive to the needs of the slow learner in his classes and the weaker members of his party.

(4)Competent leader - instructors should be constantly on the lookout for more knowledge and strive to verify it. Information gained first hand through years of personal experience and intimate contact with nature may be highly valued.

The Taking of Game:

When the student has mastered the basic skills of fire lighting, shelter construction, navigation, the use of tools, backpacking and first aid; then living off the land may be appropriate. Game laws do not generally allow for this activity and gaining permission to do so may not be easy.

It is recommended to go hungry for a while to experience its effects and try to live off wild edible plants to prove to yourself how much of a challenge it can be. In some forms of modern survival training to live off the land is not indulged in until clothing, fire, shelter, first aid, navigation and fasting are mastered. A normal healthy person may survive 40 days without eating. If you do not know well enough what you are doing you will die sooner as has been observed on many occasions.

Fire skills:

It may appear that excessive emphasis is placed on fire skills in the Boreal forest. As this ecology is amply supplied with fuel there is no need to skimp. Big fires are necessary when the cold is pervasive and brutal. The heavy use of big campfires in parks of any kind is frowned upon. The benefits of fire for restoring body warmth, drying clothing, warming shelters, cooking, providing hot drinks, sterilizing, providing light at night, for smoke signals, being a morale booster, warding off insects, and so on makes it an important aspect of Boreal survival. The modern backpacker is inclined to forego these benefits perhaps because of their tendency to use parks.

Fire is hazardous if used improperly; forest fires can be caused by carelessness. A fire that is appropriate on one day may be dangerous in the same location on another day. Even a matter of a few hours may compromise safety, as when dew evaporates and grass becomes dry at the beginning of a hot day.

Drying Clothes:

Drying clothes using a small fire is a slow process that may result in the scorching of some part. Build a large fire, to dry large areas and stand back at least three steps to avoid scorching anything.

Classroom work:

People are not as interested in theory at the beginning of a course as much as instructors might imagine. Delve deeper into theory at the end of the course when it seems to be better appreciated. Assume that the attention span of most people is short; break up your lecture by alternating lecturing with hands on activities. Frequently recap the important knowledge.

- o Introduce yourself and give a good account of your background relevant to the course.
- o Be on time, early enough to arrange seating, etc.
- o Explain what you are going to do on the course
- o Be polite
- o Speak clearly towards the students

- o Avoid using notes, except for occasional reference

Some General Points:

- Usually a lecture starts when all the registered students are present. Often one student is late (as sooner or later happens to all of us) holding up the rest who have been on time. The remedy is to start with a secondary topic for the benefit of those on time and switch to the main topic when the laggard arrives. This benefits those that are on time and the laggard does not miss out on anything important. Inform your students of this process.

- Have the students introduce themselves for your benefit and the rest of the class. Have them provide a bit of their background. Some may be skilled at something like first aid.
- The students may learn as much from their fellow course takers as they do from you. Provide them some opportunity to do so.
- A smartly dressed personal appearance gains respect from your class or group.
- Relax and look as if you enjoy your work.
- Cultivate a graceful way to recognize and turn to the benefit of the class any positive contribution from any student.
- Always try to answer any questions promptly. If you are not sure you have the answer, admit it.
- Provide a mid-morning and mid-afternoon break.
- Pay attention to the clock to start and quit on time.

YOU EXPLAIN AND DEMONSTRATE THE STUDENT IMITATES AND PRACTICES

a. The Aim of the lesson should be stated.
b. The instructor EXPLAINS and DEMONSTRATES where and when appropriate.
c. The class should IMITATE the actions under the instructor's control step by step.
d. The class then PRACTICES with the instructor supervising.
e. The instructor should have a period for QUESTIONS both from and to the class.
f. Finally, the instructor should SUMMARIZE what has been taught.

THE LEADER

1. A Leader must always be aware of the heavy responsibility associated with the role.
2. Safety is foremost in your mind.
3. The leader must have enough skill and experience to stay in complete charge during the trip.
4. With a newly formed group, tension and stress might be high. The leader must expect this and know how to reduce it.
5. The leader should expect such problems as blisters, frostbite, weakness, and so on that should be dealt with immediately.
6. At the start the trip the leader must inform someone with a sense of responsibility, such as a family member, RCMP or Park Warden in the National Park on:

    a. Where you are going, in detail with any possible digressions. Indicate the trail head where the vehicles will be parked.
    b. Expected time of return and by which time to assume help is needed.
    c. The names of the members in the group.
    d. Safety equipment taken. Provide a boot impression of each member of the party made with aluminum foil on carpeting.

7. A leader must be capable of displaying a considerable amount of patience.

THE HAZARDS TO GROUP MEMBERS THAT A LEADER SHOULD BE SENSITIVE TO:

1. Cold weather and strong winds – the role of clothing, fire and shelter.
2. Hypothermia and frostbite should not be allowed to happen.

3. Inadequate clothing especially footwear
4. Poor physical condition is always to be expected.
5. Inadequate equipment, ill-fitting or easily broken.
6. Too heavy packs that should be dealt with before setting out.

GROUP BRAINSTORMING FOR GROUP DECISIONS

1. State the problem to be solved as clearly as possible. Try to narrow down to specific problems. Deal with each in turn.
2. Rule out criticism.
3. Free wheel – The wilder the ideas the better It is easier to tame down an idea than enhance it.
4. The more ideas the better the chance of hitting upon a winner.
5. Attempt a combination and improvement of some of ideas that have been brought up.
6. Write down all ideas.
7. Discourage a perfectionist attitude
8. Ideally use a group of at least 12 participants, avoid breaking up into smaller groups than that.

POINTERS WHILE ON THE MOVE AND ON WALK-ABOUTS

Stay in the Lead

By being in the front you can control the pace and be able to choose stops in advance to allow you to group your people in the most advantageous way. At any stop walk back past half of your group, informing those at the head of the line to stay where they are and position yourself so that they all can hear and see. When finished have the group wait until you assume the head of the line before they begin walking again.

Face Your Group

While on the move, if you carry on a conversation with those nearest you, those behind will be stretching to hear especially if covering things relevant to the course. Tend to do your briefing only when stopped and everyone can see what you are talking about.

Provide Visibility

When talking about objects near the ground likely those closest to you are the only ones that get a good view. Try to limit yourself to points large enough to be easily observed by the whole group. Tightly packed groups obscure almost everything. Have the group get in the habit to form a large enough circle or semicircle a few feet away to increase ease of viewing. The group should generally have their backs to the sun.

Speak Loudly Enough

Make sure everyone can hear you but adjust your volume to the group's size. Questions should be repeated for the benefit of the entire group or your reply may be meaningless to those who didn't hear the original query.

Occasionally Take Breaks to Be Still

Stop at particularly interesting or scenic spots. Provide the appropriate explanation and give the group sufficient time to quietly absorb and meditate.

Use Teachable Moments to Advantage

There occur unexpectedly and spontaneously.

Set a Reasonable Pace

First get a little away from camp then tend to the inevitable last adjustments. Set a pace which will not tire the slower participants and avoid creating large gaps in the group as you travel. Position the slowest person behind the leader. On long stretches with no complex navigation let this person take the lead to set the pace.

For Those Who Struggle

Keep a close look out for those who are struggling with something or other and try to resolve any problems as soon as they are detected.

Keep a Head Count

On extended hikes, especially in rougher terrain, frequent head counts should be taken. Appoint a tail end person behind whom no one is allowed to fall behind.

Emergencies

Heart attacks, bee stings, asthma episodes, sprains, bruises, and simple exhaustion sometimes compounded by heat or cold may happen. Develop contingency plans to cover all possible emergency situations that you can imagine. With modern communication available, there is merit in carrying a cell phone and appoint someone as the contact person who should be made familiar with your situation who can immediately rally the resources to come to your aid. Many activities are undertaken without adequate provision of communication when in this day and age very little effort is required to provide it. Whatever the case, plan ahead and be trained in enough of the first aid measures that may have to be taken. A group first aid kit to supplement what each person carries and a group bear spray should be included on all walks and hikes. Always think – if detained overnight how well will I manage with what I have brought with me.

Children

Youngsters are usually attracted to the group leader or interpreter. They may vie with each other to see who can remain closest to the interpreter, almost stepping all over that individual in their zeal. Loosing shoe heels is a hazard in this occupation. Usually less inhibited than their older peers, they often slip their hand into yours. They may be a nuisance but to them you are a hero. If they like you and you obviously like them, you win their parents as a bonus. Develop the skill to handle these situations gracefully.

Officially End Your Session

Avoid causing an uncertain end to your walk, talk or lecture. A concluding statement should neatly wrap up any loose ends, ask for questions and summarize what was covered or accomplished, and state that the session has ended, thanking them for their participation.

Views on the 'Certification' of Survival Instructors

Based on the work of Professor Claude Cousineau – University of Ottawa

The purpose of certification is to be an incentive to improve the quality and the safety of survival training, as opposed to providing professional status or a licensing procedure for employment.

The present social conditions (i.e. accountability, safety conscientiousness and malpractice lawsuits) will force us to be 'officially' competent whether we like it or not.

Survival instructors should not be placed in a position where they will be forced to show their 'credentials'. They should not wait for the pressure of the government, concerned citizens, the insurance companies, and the general public to become organized. The initiative should come from the survival instructors themselves. The profession of medicine did not wait for the law to intervene. The physicians developed their own criteria of competency in order to protect the public and their profession. Who is better equipped to develop standards of competency in outdoor survival instruction than the people already involved in survival instruction?

Certification in survival instruction should be on a voluntary basis. In other words, no one should be forced to become certified in order to 'practice'.

Society would feel much better if it could be reassured that some control of the instructors is exercised. But there is a great danger that a measure, such as certification, becomes just another comfortable illusion. This brings another question: *Do the survival instructors wish to certify themselves simply for the 'look' or to enhance the quality and the safety of survival instruction?*

It would be fair to assume that a comprehensive certification system would improve the quality and safety of survival instruction programs. But in the process it could reduce the number of programs run by instructors who do not have the incentive, time or resources to become certified.

Some very serious concerns and opinions can be formulated which deserve a great deal of attention. The time has not yet been reached to implement a complex certification program. The idea needs to mature and be nurtured.

More dialogue and time is required before any decision is made.

Certification, like many other social adjustments, has to go through a series of steps. Initially there is a curiosity about the issue, then there is resistance or hostility, later on there is an attempt to solve the problem. Each step should take its course.

In the area of survival training certification standards should be designed and administered by survival instructors themselves as opposed to any government agency.

An agency comprised of outdoor educators has the obligation to identify the level of competence of its practitioners.

A survival instructor should accept the overall responsibility for the learning, welfare, and safety of the participants that he instructs. He or she are the ones that must intervene and act in the case of an emergency.

A certified survival instructor should be described as a person judged competent in conducting a safe and quality experience with a group of people.

Competency development of survival instruction programs are made up of a variety of components (training, experience, leadership ability, skill, personality, health, etc.)

One should be able to become certified through the process of challenge without necessarily having to take a formal prescribed course or clinic.

There are a variety of ways to achieve competency. Not all people should necessarily have the same type of background in terms of experience and training. Diversity of instruction is desirable.

There should be a variety of ways and places to get training and experience. Simply attending a school, clinic, workshop, etc. should not be considered sufficient for certification. A certification granting agency should not necessarily be responsible for training candidates. Training and certification are two separate functions that may best be met by separate agencies.

A certification scheme in survival instruction training should make use, as much as possible, of existing tests and standards of achievement adopted by other bodies rather than to develop new ones (e.g., Red Cross, St. John Ambulance, CRCA canoeing levels).

Each component of competency should be made quantifiable in order to maintain a certain degree of objectivity.

Selection of the instrument to evaluate each component of the competency should be done in consultation with the survival instructors who will be affected by the decision.

The establishment of minimum standards of achievement for each component of competency should be done in consultation with the survival instructors who will be affected by the decision.

Compensation of one competency for another one should be possible.

In order to become certified, a candidate should have to meet a minimum standard of achievement in each area of competency and meet a higher minimum when all the components are tabulated.

As components of competency in outdoor survival instruction the following have merit:

– Successful completion of formal course clinics, workshops, etc. in outdoor survival skills.

- Experience as a leader of outdoor adventure activities and survival training.

- Experience as a leader, teacher or instructor with any kind of group experiencing any kind of learning activities.

- A list of desired personality traits for instructorship and leadership in outdoor living skills.

- A minimum age (should be established).

- Be physically healthy and fit.

- Have knowledge and skill in wilderness first aid, life-saving and rescue.

- As a condition for certification where adventurous aquatic activities are involved, a candidate should have a current certificate in life saving.

A certificate in outdoor survival instruction could also specify the areas of competency in activities such as canoe tripping, rock climbing, sailing, orienteering, caving, winter camping, cross-country skiing, white water canoeing and kayaking.

The certification scheme should include different levels of achievement in order for one to progress through a ranking system, and also be able to distinguish a number of levels of attainment between the novice and the most competent instructor (of instructors).

The examination should include fitness tests, specific outdoor skill tests, and written knowledge concerning first aid, rescue procedures, group processes, learning and teaching methodology, etc.

The concept of certification is an emotional one. Some feel threatened while others feel that it would be another societal control of which there is already an abundance. Some naively think that certification would solve the problems of outdoor adventure education while others feel that it would create more problems.

For an employee, certification signifies that he cannot be trusted until he has shown his 'paper'. For the employer, it signifies that he cannot use his own judgment in the hiring process, but that he has to rely on the judgment of others.

(Leadership in Mountain Terrain)

Good Leadership Skills:

Experience implies considerable time spent in putting yourself through the paces for assuming the status of leader. You have attended courses, taken many trips so that you feel you have mastered the necessary skills. You have a trait of character that makes you feel you would enjoy passing your knowledge on to others. The good leader should usually be the most technically skilled and competent person in the group who also has a drive to aspire to leadership.

In having to make a judgment the leader thinks through all options, and then tries to make a good decision, hopefully with a group consensus.

You must consider the strengths and weakness of your party, the environmental challenges, and the worth of your objectives you are aiming for. When a leader is appointed it is important this leadership remain clear.

A group should not normally be split on the trail. If a split becomes necessary the leader may appoint a deputy to manage the (smaller) group which may proceed at a different pace.

The leader should make conscious decisions, tending not to let anything happen by default.

The planning that goes into a trip plays an important role in determining its outcome. It should consider time, food, route, party size, injury enroute and the likely alternatives if something should force a change of plan. Analyze what could possibly force a change of plans.

If possible consult with someone who has made the trip before and try to derive some benefit from their advice.

Study all the pertinent maps at home until they are almost memorized to have a mental map that will then go everywhere with you. Observe the lay of the land, memorize landmarks and look behind now and then as you may find it useful going back.

Relate to the terrain on your map and carefully maintain the position of your party on it.

Animal trails often provide the easiest route, keeping in mind they usually begin nowhere and end nowhere. Abandon them if they digress too much from your intended route.

Understanding the geology of the area has its merit to have some idea where the steepest slopes and dangerous cliffs are located.

Watch the weather - (mid-summer) lightning storms and high altitude blizzards may occur. Study how to deal with lightening at high altitude.

River and Sand or Gravel Bar:

Although there are many obvious advantages in camping on or near a river, there are many disadvantages. The greatest hazard is flooding. In mountainous regions, flooding can be sudden, swift, and unpredictable. A man sleeping on a river bar may not awaken in time to hear it coming. The steeper the river bed, the more torrential the flood. If it is deemed necessary to camp on a river bar, choose the higher bars with an easy access to shore. Avoid camping on bars altogether if it is raining or if snow is melting on the mountains especially in late May and early June. Be aware of the consequences of camping below a hydro dam and the increased flows brought on by peak power demands that takes time to make its way down stream.

You may have to camp on a river bar to avoid insects, or to be seen by rescue aircraft, or to avoid forest fire under very dry conditions. Assess what a river may do by examining its banks for evidence of the flood water line, and the size of the drainage area (as determined from a map).

Flash floods:

Deep, long canyons (as on the Nahanni) may be subject to flash flooding caused by thunder storms unheard and unseen beyond the horizon.

Falling Rock:

Avoid camping near steep talus or cliffs, especially from which its rocks have obviously fallen or could easily be dislodged. Torrential rains can dislodge rocks or cause landslides Groups ascending or descending steep slopes must do so at enough of an angle so that no one is directly above or below anyone else to be killed by accidentally dislodged rocks. Avoid building fires against rock overhangs or faces as the expansion by the heat may cause the rock to break away.

Falling Trees and Limbs:

This applies especially to old burned over areas with large

trees. Avoid obviously leaning trees, trees struck by lightning, or any dead, heavy timber. With unusually strong winds when you hear the random crash of a tree here and there move out of range of any larger tree or into a clearing if in a forest. Large black poplar trees are notorious for shedding heavy limbs.

Quicksand or Quickmud:

Quicksand is a rare condition in the North Temperate Zone most likely to be found in mountainous terrain or where springs tend to form or below some beaver dams. Immediately on stepping into quicksand one should fall flat and swim or roll out of the area. Quicksand or mud do not create suction. Soil of this condition offers little support to weight concentrated on small areas, so a standing person will easily sink. To help remove a stuck person, build a raft out to him to support the person trying to give help, like shrubs bundled in a tarp, and pass a rope under his armpits. Apply a slow gentle pull while the victim wiggles as much as possible.

Horses should be removed out of quicksand or mud as quickly as possible as they have difficulty breathing if in neck-deep. Pass a rope around the neck and use the Spanish windlass. Cattle may be pulled out the same way but may be dangerous as they may attack rescuers out of panic.

Crossing Streams:

The crossing of streams is one of the leading killers of outdoor recreationists. Today you may cross a stream that is knee deep. A few days later in crossing it back the flow is doubled in depth to be belly button high. The moving force of the water has now increased 40 to 60 fold. Therein lies the danger.

Preparedness:

Wilderness mishaps are due to various causes singly or combined:

1. Carelessness and blunders as in navigation or reading the weather.
2. Over estimation of physical stamina.
3. Over estimation of one's technical ability.
4. Misinformation – things that were supposed to be there are not.
5. Lack of knowledge and experience on how to make oneself comfortable enough to sleep if detained in the bush.

When going into the bush you should be prepared for the unexpected. True self sufficiency allows one to cope with any unexpected delay by providing your own rations, the means for keeping warm enough to sleep, doing your own navigating and route finding, being able to recognize wilderness hazards in time to avoid them and also have the knowledge to manage without (lost) equipment or the lack of food. Most people get into trouble by overextending experience, knowledge, physical capability and mental stamina. Realize that many of the predicaments encountered in the bush have to be anticipated and planned for to be effectively dealt with or avoided.

Inexperience in the Mountains:

A nearby mountain can be a strong attraction and a definite hazard to one unfamiliar with the dangers that might be encountered walking to the summit.

1. Mountain storms can come on very suddenly. Being caught on the mountain in a snow storm you may have to stop moving to avoid a lethal fall or deal with a lightning storm.

2. One can underestimate the time it takes to get to the summit and run out of time to get down safely in daylight.
3. Descending by too steep a slope with possible injury or broken bones.
4. Descending by a different route from the one used to ascend and encountering an even steeper slope, a cliff, or an overhang.
5. Neglecting to bring water or carbohydrates to provide the energy demanded by mountain travel.
6. Not realizing the possibility and effects of becoming giddy from the rarefied air.
7. Lacking the resources (clothing and equipment) for an (uncomfortable) stay overnight.
8. Not realizing the mountaintop is much colder than the balmy valley.

Inexperience in Cross Country Skiing:

Someone goes out for an extended trip on skis when it is very cold out. A ski breaks or a binding comes apart due to the loss of screws. A planned 5 hour outing is now extended to 24 because the person cannot make a repair or devise a substitution. Does he know enough and is adequately equipped to be found alive the next morning? Inexperience and not being sensitive to the possible problems is the main cause for the 'survival' situation. Would he know enough about snow shelter building or the use of fire to get by that night in the cold. Skiing involves speed which can bring on a sudden severe injury that immobilizes the victim who is now lying in the snow. Ski clothing is relatively light in keeping with the physical exertion encountered in that activity.

Inexperience in Canoeing:

When canoeing you suddenly realize there is a situation ahead you want to avoid. Can you stop the canoe's movement relative to the banks and then go to either one using the current to get you there?

When being blown off a lake shore by an unexpected strong wind do you know enough to paddle against it by having the rear paddler move up behind the bow paddler until the canoe naturally weathervanes into the wind to be paddled back to shore?

Eating:

a) Poisonous Plants:

In attempting to live off the wild edible plants never eat any part of any unknown plant. Eat only wholesome, properly prepared plants that are positively identified. To use plants in a medicinal way, internally, is asking for trouble (unless you are a practicing expert). Local poisonous plants should be studied until they are easily recognized. These plants should be known by their scientific name if possible. In cases of suspected poisoning by any plant, medical help should be sought immediately and the correct name of the plant be provided. When the victim is taken to the hospital, gather substantial samples of the offending plant to go with him for identification. Parts of the plant may be found in the victims vomit or mouth.

b) Spoiled Food:

When you realize you have eaten something that might be poisonous the state of mind that results is something you never want to ever experience again.

(i) Clostridium Group: Canned food that gives off an odor or appears unusual in any way should not be tasted in case it is affected by clostridium botulinum, a particularly virulent bacterium of which a very small amount can be lethal. Boiling for at least 15 minutes destroys the toxin, if it is suspected.

Symptoms of poisoning will usually appear from 12 to 36 hours of ingestion. Vomiting, constipation, dizziness, weakness, headache, fever, and visual difficulties are followed by (creeping) paralysis, especially of the eye, throat and chest muscles. Seek medical attention immediately, bringing samples of the offending food.

(ii) Salmonella Group: Incubation period of salmonella 6 to 48 hours, usually showing effects at 12 hours after ingestion. Onset is abrupt with headache, chills, fever, muscle aches, and prostration accompanied with nausea, vomiting, abdominal cramps, and severe diarrhea that last 24 to 48 hours.

(iii) Trichinosis: The hazard of consuming the flesh of a carnivore. Undercooking meat, especially bear meat, may be inviting trichinosis. Some signs are colicky pains, nausea, and diarrhea, which are later followed by muscular pain, dyspnea, fever and edema.

c) Contaminated Water:

Water suspected to be contaminated should be kept at a boil for a minimum of five minutes as a simplistic rule of thumb used by the author as sterilizing water in the Boreal Forest is not as serious as may be encountered in other environments, it is not dealt with in depth here. Recommended amounts of Halazone, Chlorine Dioxide, or other chemical treatment per quart of water may make the water safe in half an hour. A temporary water supply may be established by digging a shallow well near enough to a lake, pond, stream or It is difficult to predict where contaminated water may be encountered. Northern hospitals have difficulty in disposing of their wastes so always purify any water downstream. Water from muskeg lakes may have a strong moldy taste. This may be removed by including a few pieces of charcoal while boiling.

d) Overeating After a Long Fast or Starvation:

This can bring on severe digestive upset causing further exhaustion and weakness. If available, skim milk should be given in moderate quantities at first and only after the victim is able to assimilate it well, he is then given small quantities of other foods, like potatoes boiled to a mush or the baby food called pablum.

Thawed Foods:

Meat: If meat has thawed completely and smell and color seem normal, it can be well cooked immediately and eaten. The meat may also be refrozen, especially if it contains ice crystals or it may be cooked to extend its storage life for a few days. It is best to avoid altogether meat that seems only 'slightly' spoiled.

Vegetables: Vegetables that still have ice crystals may be refrozen, canned or cooked and eaten immediately. Any frozen vegetables put into boiling water will cook as if they have never been frozen. If thawed they turn to mush.

Poultry and Fish: Poultry and fish should be discarded if there is the slightest sign of spoilage. It is difficult to tell by odor or color if spoilage has begun. The decision to use or discard should be based on how long it has been kept in warm conditions. Many bacteria can live at low temperatures. If ice crystals are present the meat can be refrozen immediately.

Etiquette in the Bush

Living in the bush with others may demand some points of etiquette that are not immediately apparent – at least that is the author's impression after many years of conducting courses in the bush.

It takes time to realize what aspects of one's conduct are annoying to others.

1. Help the cook: The cook is king or queen as the gender may be. Regardless of the normal disposition of the camp cook, it will always improve if he or she never has to fetch water or firewood. If you have time to spare, offer your services to help keep the cooking fire stoked, wash dishes or peel potatoes. There have been a number of times when I have been told by the cook that I must be the only real bushman in the camp on account of these small considerations.
2. Stoking the fire: When the stew is being cooked over the fire do not heap on the firewood without making the cook aware of what you are doing.
3. Cooking duties: If it's your turn to cook, wash your hands and clean your fingernails. While in the bush, there is as much, if not more need to wash your hands after going to the toilet as there is in 'civilization'.
4. Toilet decorum: Cleanliness and neatness of persons are desirable quirks of character in the out of doors. However, good manners indicate that washing, cleaning the fingernails, brushing of teeth, blowing the nose fiercely, are more appropriately done a respectable distance from the campfire, but not necessarily completely out of sight.
5. Do not spit: If you are in good health you do not need to spit, even in the out of doors. Some people seem to spit out of habit more so around the campfire than anywhere else. Seeing someone spitting on the ground or into the fire in camp is an acute turn-off for many people. If you need to clear your throat, it should be away from the general campsite or into something disposable and gotten rid of by burning or burial.
6. Do your laundry: Stale clothing and body odor are as difficult to stand in the bush as anywhere else. You should be able to launder clothing with reasonable ease in the bush. Your bush living skills are incomplete if you

do not know how to return to civilization as clean as you left it.

7. Do not step over pots and plates: Do not step over food, be it a plate or pot as this almost always causes foreign matter to fall into the food.

8. Rubbish: Do not burn rubbish, especially plastics, while food is cooking or while people are eating as such disagreeable odors are hard to breathe in at any time. Paper ash may get into the stew or other's food. Burning cans may impart a metallic taste to food being cooked over the same fire. The by-products of combustion of any plastic are quite unpleasant to breathe in.

9. Dishes: Do not leave dirty (or clean) dishes underfoot. If washing your own dishes is the camp custom, take care of this chore immediately on completion of any meal. Generally it is excusable to do away with most eating utensils – to use a pint sauce pan instead of a plate, bowl and mug and a large spoon instead of a fork and spoon

10. Carry a small mirror: In dusty conditions pay particular attention to the corners of the eyes or mouth when washing. After meals, check to make sure there is no food on your face.

11. Borrowing: Do not ask to borrow someone's knife, axe or saw. If a job has to be done, and you don't have the required tool, ask the owner to do it for you. This may so astonishing they may likely lend you the tool.

12. Following too closely: When on the trail, if the branches from the person ahead of you are slapping you in the face, it is your own fault for following too closely.

13. Visitors: When visitors happen upon your camp, it is the custom to offer tea at the least.

14. Snoring: If you are a loud snorer, or prone to considerable flatulence, you should have the good manners to set up your own camp an appropriate distance away. Think far enough ahead to provide your own shelter to do so

The ultimate in good manners: Good manners dictate that all vulgarity, mishaps, blunders and accidents on the part of others be tolerated without comment with a philosophical indifference. Tenderfeet need time to learn.

Safe River Crossing

River crossing is dangerous. Many people perish from the hazard of crossing rivers; a leading killer of outdoor recreationists. Reading moving water, river features and stream development processes can assist in the selection of safe crossings and to help choose the applicable techniques.

The critical elements are distance, water immersion times, and wind. Swimming such distances with a pack would be foolhardy.

Moving water is affected by the characteristics of its riverbed. Mountain rivers are seldom flat and straight. Bad composition, channel width, depth, gradient and direction all influence waters often following a circuitous path downstream under the force of gravity. Reconnaissance of the selected crossing point may consider several of the following:

Current Speed – In straight unobstructed channels, water flows faster in the center and slower at the bottom and edges through friction. As water flows fastest on the outside bends and slowest on the inside and the likeliness of steep banks and possible undertows caused by helical currents.

Pillows – Mid-stream boulders or rocks produce visible effects on an otherwise smooth surface. Low water volumes may not completely cover boulders, to create a 'pillow' on the upstream side, providing the boulder is not undercut. Deal with this feature by pushing off with the feet when in the recommended swimming position.

Effects of Increased Flow Rates – Increased flows can wash-out certain hydraulics while others become increasingly violent. Be prepared for the worst. A steeper riverbed followed by a flat section causes water to recirculate over itself as the volume of water cannot be accommodated fast enough downstream in the calmer water resulting in 'holes' or 'stoppers'

Avoid strong water flows. Some common forms of ledges creating strong water flows across river channels are as follows:

Downstream and Upstream Vees – The clearest passages are between obstructions that mark chutes. Vees pointing upstream are usually caused by rocks. Aim for the downstream pointing vees if you have any choice in the matter.

Stacks – Stacks occur at the apex of downstream vees where fast, deep water converges. Although most do not have an obstruction within them to hurt a swimmer, be aware that some are upstream curling waves concealing close-to-surface boulders.

Eddies – Rocks obstructing the channel or extending from shore may be used to advantage by providing rest stops especially on wide channels. In shallow rivers the downstream currents are dissipated behind protruding rocks where the water flows in from the edges and downstream creating a pocket of relatively calm water moving upstream.

River Hazards –

Sweepers – Keep clear of sweepers that may trap you in their tangle. Above water sweepers may be concealing more beneath the surface than can be spotted from the shore.

Log Jams – Could be useful for crossing but may be lethal if you manage to fall through.

Foot Entrapments – Careless foot placements even in shallow water can trap feet in vertically faulted bedrock or between boulders. It does not take much of a current to force your body and head below the surface.

Stream Evolution –

Study how to select crossings from maps and aerial photographs.

Useful Considerations for Stream Crossings –

Temperature – Cold air and water. Hypothermia is a real threat.

Time of day – Consider glacial and snow melt, hydroelectric power dam demands.

Downstream obstructions – Is there a back up if the target is missed.

Cross-river communications – Is a signal system necessary?

Footing security – Icy, mossy, bare and dry?

Group preparedness – Mental alertness in the event of an accident.

Water turbidity – Clear, glacial silt laden?

Sound of boulders rolling in the current?

Recent heavy rains – Wait for the level to drop.

SAFETY

Safety is uppermost in planning a river crossing. Do you really have to cross this river? What happens if I fall in or be swept away? How strong a swimmer are you on injury, how quickly could help arrive? Are there party members who will have difficulty with this crossing, even though you can negotiate it easily? Assess all the risks and only then make your decision. Fatalities occur when poor judgment and bad crossing techniques are combined with dangerous water conditions.

Where river crossing is commonly engaged in, there is considerable merit in subjecting the group to preliminary training to develop proficiency and feel before serious crossings are undertaken.

Crossing on foot:

Cautions: If you are in a hurry to cross a river, you are asking for trouble before you have even stepped into the water. Never cross flooded rivers – the risk is too great. You should never cross a river when trees are floating down it or boulders are heard rolling in it. Wait until the river subsides. When the snow is melting (especially in the second or third week of June in the eastern Canadian Rockies) crossing a river may be the most dangerous part of a trip. The character of a river may change completely with a few inches rise in water level. Each time the depth doubles, the velocity also doubles. On each doubling the water can shift objects forty to sixty times greater in weight previous to the doubling. Skill at crossing rivers is acquired through experience and practice. Those who need to cross rivers should gain the necessary experience by practicing in a river or part of a river where it is safe to do so. You first have to overcome the feeling of dizziness caused by the moving water.

With practice, most people become used to this feeling. The middle of a stream that is trying to sweep your feet away is a poor place to start getting used to this feeling.

New Zealanders have a rule of thumb to gauge the feasibility of a crossing. If the depth and velocity of the water, multiplied together, exceed the value of one in meters and seconds, the crossing is too hazardous. For example: half a meter deep times two meters per second is a limiting value. Estimating a river's speed is critical because its power obviously increases with velocity. In rocky rivers, turbulence also increases with speed, and foaming, highly aerated water offers little buoyancy while one is being swept away.

Poor swimmers are obviously very vulnerable. Crossing rivers with cold spring melt water is inviting problems with cold immersion hypothermia. Water conducts heat from a warm human twenty times faster than in air of the same temperature. A fully clothed adult will lapse into unconsciousness in 20 minutes when immersed in water at 5°C and dies in 30 minutes. A few seconds immersion causes a loss of manual coordination, grip strength and touch discrimination.

Choice of Ford:

1. You should take time to study a considerable stretch of the river to find a safe crossing.
2. Find a high spot to survey large sections of river to get a better appraisal on the gradient, turbulence, width of the river, and the nature of its bottom.
3. The river bank often gives clues as to what the bottom may be composed of. A smooth gravel bottom is the most desirable.
4. Look for a widening in the river as the water will usually be shallower and flow slower.
5. There is often shallower water just before a change in gradient of a river (above rapids).

6. A broad part of the river or one that breaks up into many braids is usually easier to cross.
7. Avoid curves as the water is deeper and stronger on the outside of the bends.
8. A point halfway between a bend and its reverse is a good place for your crossing.
9. The river below the crossing should also be safe. In the event that your footing is lost, or legs broken, equipment loss or drowning could result. A safe run out may facilitate a rescue.
10. The entrance and exit of a ford should be easy to navigate.
11. The nature of a river bottom can change beyond recognition in a short time. Assume nothing. Treat a familiar crossing as if you are seeing it for the first time.
12. In the mountains, the rise in water level can fluctuate considerably. Rain in catchment areas results in a rise shortly after. Streams fed by melting snow will be at their lowest in the early morning.
13. Camping and starving on a riverbank may be far more desirable than death by drowning.

Before Crossing:

Are you sure that you can cope with a dunking?

1. **DO NOT REMOVE FOOTWEAR.** Without footwear it is difficult to find a secure placement of foot and it is far easier to lose your balance and injure your feet. It is permissible to remove socks and insoles.
2. Pants, however, should either be tight fitting or be removed because they offer a great deal of drag.
3. Heavy coats, parkas, etc., should not be worn as they will prove very cumbersome when wet.
4. The weight of your pack should give you added purchase against the current. Likewise, being carried across may be useful to consider. Undo the waistband on your pack, so it will be easier to drop your pack.

Crossing with one shoulder strap undone will contribute to your unbalance.

5. Close up your pack to make it as waterproof as possible. Enclosing everything in waterproof plastic bags, especially sleeping bags, will enable your pack to provide flotation in the event of a mishap. On losing your footing float your pack ahead of you using it for balance. If you can't hold on to your pack, let it go. It will likely come ashore downstream.

6. In deep water, a pack may be better held in front of you. On your back it may not hold your head above water.

Crossing Alone:

Question your sanity when you choose to travel alone where river crossing is necessary.

1. A staff can be used on the upstream side to help to maintain your balance as well as probing for obstructions. Use a staff to two and a half meters long. A staff acts as a third leg, improving your stability. Place the pole slightly ahead and upstream so that the water forces the tip against the bottom. Lift the pole clear of the water to a new position and then move up to it. Present your body sideways to the current to minimize the drag. Assume a ferry glide position with the hips. Rotate with the current.

2. Carefully shuffle along feeling for the bottom with your feet. Once one foot is firmly placed move the other foot, keep your feet apart and never allow them to cross. Beware of the possibility of trapping your foot in narrow gaps. Beware of slippery algae-covered stones. Drag your feet – avoid lifting them. Push movable stones aside.

3. Avoid looking down at the water swirling around you. Fix your gaze onto the point you are walking toward.

4. The crossing may be made easier by allowing the current to carry you a little diagonally downstream. Take

advantage of eddies to rest. Going from eddy to eddy will ease the strain of an entire crossing.

5. How deep you go depends on the swiftness of the current. You may reach a point where it is impossible to maintain your footing.

6. Never face downstream when alone as the force of the water against the back of the knees will tend to buckle them. With three people the middle person should face downstream. With larger groups a few should face downstream for providing added stability. Keep one side of your body into the current to reduce the amount of surface exposed to the flow. If your footing is lost and you feel yourself being swept away, turn to face downstream and take big strides to regain some control, to get past obstacles and to return to shore. If you are being carried by the water, lead with your feet so that you can fend off rocks and boulders. When you are crossing alone it is especially important that run out is safe.

7. Control any panic. Keep your head, determine where safety lies and methodically work in that direction. Work slowly and let the current do most of the work. It helps to know how moving water works and use it to advantage.

Group Crossing:

1. A green pole up to 8 centimeters in diameter can be used for groups of 3 to 6 people.

2. The pole is clasped firmly against the chest with the upstream arm under the pole and the downstream arm over the pole.

3. If only a thin pole is available everyone could interlock arms.

4. The weakest people are placed in the middle of the group.

5. No one should let go in case of a slip because each person contributes to the safety of the whole group.

6. The pole must always be kept in line with the flow of the water. Never turn in midstream.
7. If a decision is made to retreat and walking backwards is impossible, then one individual at a time should try changing position or direction.

Rope Crossing:

Used prudently, ropes can take you across a river that otherwise would not be crossable. But used without proper preparation or used carelessly, they can be deadly. A simple hand line is one of the most commonly used methods. For this crossing, the rope should be run diagonally across the water instead of straight across one shore to the other, so that a vee won't form in the center of the rope and trap a person in the point of the vee. When crossing on a hand line, you can use a carabineer with a sling attached to the chest. Waders can also simply hold onto the downstream side of the rope (on the upstream side, a fall could get you entangled in the rope), and move across hand-over-hand.

1. A rope twice as long as the river is wide is required. When planning for crossing, carry 150 feet of 5 millimeter climbing-type rope.
2. The most adept person crosses with one end of the rope at a point where a safe run out will allow them to be swept back to shore with the assistance of the rope.
3. A loop is made in the middle of the rope and the second person to cross is tied around the waist or chest.
4. The first person ties the end to an immovable object, or at worst their own waist. A third person ties the rope's end around his or her waist and plays it out as needed. The first person takes it up. If the first person stands a ways upstream, should the person crossing stumble, the belayer (first person) will more or less be swung into shore.

5. When the rope is submerged, there is considerable drag put on it by the current. Remaining members could go as far as possible into the water and hold the rope above their heads or set up tripods for this purpose.
6. The person crossing should endeavor to make it without being pulled. A pull by either the first or third person will surely pull them off balance and then the two of them have far more work to do.
7. The first person to cross should build a good fire for those coming across to get warmed up and dried. A steam bath on both sides may be a good idea.

Rope Stretched Across River:

This should only be used as a convenience where a very shallow river is crossed frequently and perhaps has a slippery bottom. In dangerous crossings, the rope will put you under severe strain when your foothold is lost. My Australian and New Zealand sources of information indicate this method has resulted in many fatalities.

Being Towed Across:

Especially in the case of weak members of the party, it is recommended that a deep pool is preferable to a swift rapid. Buoyant packs could be used to advantage for added support. Where a large group has to cross and the water is deep but not exceptionally swift a coracle-ferry may be appropriate.

Frozen rivers are particularly hazardous:

Springs, currents, and subsurface obstructions cause weak ice that snowdrifts can camouflage. Crossing with skis helps distribute your weight, but that doesn't assure safety. If you must make an ice traverse of a river or frozen lake, take time to test the ice ahead of you. And keep at least ten yards between yourself and your partners. Water in winter simply presents a hazard that is difficult to overstate.

Fording Streams with a Vehicle:

In the absence of a bridge or in the event of an unsafe bridge, it may be necessary to ford. Never ford a stream until the greatest depth of the water and the condition or firmness of the bottom is known. Check this information yourself as yesterday's information is no good today. Conditions vary at every crossing point, and the ordinary practical approach usually does the job without undue risk or difficulty.

The narrowest place is not always the best crossing. Search for shallow water with a good firm, gravelly bottom.

A man should be able to wade across and probe the bottom with a stick, thus locating very large rocks and deep holes.

Both banks should provide an easy entrance and exit. Usually men with hand tools must do this on the opposite bank until the first dozer is over. This is important.

Get a stout line across the stream and have a sound anchor.

It may be necessary to winch across.

Use two dozers for safety whenever possible.

If truck and dozer must both ford, put the dozer over first. He can winch the truck over if necessary.

It is usually recommended to cross at an angle; that is, down-stream and with the current.

If the water is deep, the fan belt should be loosened.

As a rule fording presents few problems, especially in the heat of summer when streams are low.

Swimming Across a River:

When you are faced with a river too deep to wade but calm
enough to swim, as ever, judgment and forethought are essential.
Are there rapids, whirlpools, rocky projections, waterfalls
downstream? What will happen if you don't make the other
shore where you planned to? Are there bends around which you
cannot see?

One technique for swimming rivers is using your pack as a
buoyant aid. Gear is packed in plastic bags, which are then
packed in a second layer of bags, and put inside the pack.
Trapped air keeps the pack afloat. Inflated ziplock bags in side
pockets add even more buoyancy.

If you do get into trouble in mid-stream, be ready to let go of
the pack if it jeopardizes your own safety. Face downstream,
float on your back with your feet up and legs extended, so that
they, and not your head, will contact boulders and logs first.
Swim across the current toward the shore closer to you.

The Keeping of a Log of Wilderness Experiences

At one time a ship's speed was determined by the use of a floating piece of wood, to which was attached a speed measuring device. The record of speed so determined was kept in a 'log' book, sometimes known as a ship's log. Eventually the term 'log' came to mean the record of any journey.

Where a log is a record of a ship's journey, the personal (bush) log is a record of one's journey through the trials and tribulations of learning something about the bush and often about one's self.

Through keeping a detailed log, individuals involved in wilderness programs should be better able to keep track of their progress and experience in bush knowledge and techniques. There are many useful courses given throughout the country that often do not result in a certificate. A proper log entry could substitute for a certificate. The national and provincial canoeing associations will likely require their members to log river trips in the near future for those who wish to progress in their ranks.

Log Content:

The log keeping suggested is for recording your experiences to prove to others their breadth and depth relevant to any aspirations to become a group leader in bush tripping or instructor in wilderness skills. Whenever you take a course, enter a reasonably detailed outline of what you observed, learned and practiced. At the end of each course, if possible, make an evaluation of what you have personally gained. Note that keeping a log is not the same as keeping notes.

If an instructor is involved he or she should sign and date your log to your discretion. A log with proper endorsements should be the strongest proof of your participation.

Any private projects you engage in should also be recorded.

For future reference a record of the following points on river tripping can prove to be of value, especially if you are a leader and intend to conduct similar trips along the same route.

Log Entries:

a. Departure and arrival times to establish an accurate idea of time required to make the trip.
b. Costs and personal commitment.
c. Nature of route, dangers, hazards, inconveniences, good camping sites, what the route may be best suited for.
d. Liabilities. Make a detailed note of the circumstances surrounding any accident, not only your own but any observed. Record noteworthy changes of personality of any participants. The more ominous the legal implications are, the more care and detail should be taken in making the log entries. The log is an important legal tool or document if it is recorded in an intact, bound book, such as made by the Dominion Blank Book Company Ltd. (No 56 1 / 2 Faint, 19.3 x 12 cm, 192 pages). Never tear pages out of a log or its legal validity

may be impaired. The following may also be entered into the log.

e. Expectations or objectives for the day, and later, how these have been fulfilled or accomplished.
f. Feelings or reactions as a result of the program, personal interactions, etc.
g. Growth in knowledge, expertise, etc.
h. Observations and comments on anything that affects participants mentally, physically, interpersonal relations, etc.
i. Any good ideas, Suggestions future projects, and plans.
j. Anything of future use that may not be trusted to the memory.

Your log is not a private diary to be hidden from others. It is essentially supposed to be a (legal) public document that you may make available to those who have a need to assess your experience in outdoor skills. Personal references to others other than their professional relationship to you should be omitted. In some situations such as psychotherapy, personal references may be a necessity, but this would be an entirely different type of log.

One of the most useful functions of the log is to determine any change in attitudes or progress in skill development. This is of special importance in the facilitation of rehabilitation or psychotherapeutic wilderness programs. Trying to prove any progress in personality development without a log may be difficult.

If the daily flow of events, mental and or physical, are not set down they soon fade from memory and being able to make before and after comparisons may be lost. The leader may set aside a specific time of day when everyone can work on their logs to assure their regular upkeep.

Depending on the program, the log may have a different emphasis. An ordinary teaching campout is going to be different from a trip with a group of young offenders or with a group of people on a wilderness challenge course.

At the beginning and end of a course, the leader should gather the group together and request that everyone (as a group perhaps) write down what they are feeling at that moment, their intended commitment, their expectations before they start and their evaluation at the end. Re-evaluation of these expectations and commitments may be done from time to time as circumstances and conditions change. The leaders may also dictate special entries at various times. For example, half way through some extensive thought may be asked for on what group interaction has contributed to the program thus far.

At the end the leader may 'de-brief'' the group by evaluating the program as to its merits and drawbacks and have participants compare their present state to that recorded earlier. The de-briefing session should be the appropriate time to ask for suggestions for improvement and to air any complaints (perhaps in such a way that the leader has the opportunity to defend himself).

The results of any exams or evaluations given might be recorded by the instructor into the individual participant's logs.

Sample entry made by individual taking a

'Short Course':

Date: Course given on June 19 and 20, 1976
Place: Blue Lake Center (Hinton) Alberta
Name of Course: Basic Natural Crafts

Content of Course:

1. Learned to identify silver willow and how to make cordage from it. I made about 4 feet of 1/8" two strand cord.
2. Learned to identify stinging nettle and made approx. 4 ft of thread from it by the twining method.
3. I learned how to select and sharpen a good knife including how to make one's own sharpening equipment.
4. Carved a 'TRY' stick to learn safe knife manipulation and the terminology for a number of carving operations.
5. Carved a netting needle and gage and netted a square meter of mesh of 5 cm. in size.
6. Carved tinder box out of black poplar bark.
7. Made a woman doll out of cattail leaves and a 'hot pot' mat by the coiling technique out of the leaves as well.
8. Made a spruce root ring (Turk's head) of roots I gathered and stripped myself.

Evaluation:

The course gave an introduction to getting started in natural crafts and the potential of naturally available materials in arts and crafts, which was a real eye opener to me. Although I was only able to accomplish the above activities, I got an insight into a lot more on such things as basket weaving, whistles and flutes, bows and arrows, general camp crafts, etc. I thoroughly enjoyed the course and must confess I knew very little of any of this before having taken it.

Instructor's Comment:

This is to verify that Susan Black took the above mentioned course and was found to be a keen and active participant. (M. Kochanski), June 20, 1976, Blue Lake Center.

The log keeper may then give an evaluation of the instructor which does not necessarily have to be seen by the instructor.

Sample entry made by group leader – instructor:

Date: October 25, 1975, 5th day out, 2000 hrs.
Weather: Cold, windy, 8° C, clear sky.
Position: On Athabasca River, approx. 30 miles below Smith River, smooth, current approx. 3 mph (based on statement of experienced canoeist), uneventful, no rapids.
Distance covered: 0800 to 1800 is 25 km.

Events:

Nothing unusual, everybody is enjoying the trip thus far. At 2020 Keanu Reeves cut right index finger with pocket knife, midway between first and second knuckle. Knife closed while attempting to drill hole through black poplar bark. 2 or 3 stitches may have been necessary. Polysporin ophthalmic ointment applied around cut and would closed with two butterfly closures and covered with a Telfa pad bound on with Elastoplast.

The long hours of paddling leave me quite tired. I do not really feel up to instructing and the students seem too tired to be interested in being instructed this evening. Everyone will have free time instead of an evening program.

Comment:

The campsite has so many wind blown spruce it is an ideal site to teach bough beds, shelters, and signal fires. A better campsite may have been passed three kilometers back, coordinates 798 341 83F 11 West half DALEHURST. (Ponoka creek on map.)

Note:

Many people include their notes in with their log. This detracts from the original intention of the log. Someone evaluating it is forced to wade through reams of unnecessary information. If you insist on mixing notes into your log then underline (in color) the information that the evaluator wants to see.

Writing Instrument:

Do not use water soluble ink as it may run if the log gets damp through rain or canoe upset. HB to 2H pencils are recommended. Keep the log in a waterproof bag.

Time to Maintain Log:

Generally a log should take less than half an hour per day to maintain. Entries must be made daily while the memory is still fresh. There is some merit for the leader having the whole group work on their logs at the same appointed time

ABOUT THE AUTHOR

Mors Kochanski is known throughout North America for his extensive work in outdoor education, survival and wilderness living.

His enthusiasm for wilderness recreation, his extensive knowledge of the field, and his desire to learn everything there is to know about the wilderness has made him one of the foremost authorities on wilderness skills.

Mors Kochanski has been an outdoor educator and survival instructor for over 40 years, twenty three of which as a sessional professor for the University of Alberta; a few months of which were at the Canadian Department of National Defense Survival School at Jarvis Lake, Alberta. For many years Mors instructed courses at the Blue Lake Centre run by the Alberta Department of Culture Youth and Recreation, and finally 17 years for the School District 59, at Dawson Creek, British Columbia to the benefit of thousands of elementary school children. All the while, this tireless scholar did copious research, freelanced as an instructor, and wrote numerous magazine articles for Alberta Wilderness Arts and Recreation Magazine, various popular aid-memoir booklets and the instant classic "Northern Bushcraft" (now known as Bushcraft).

This is just a handful of Mors' outdoor education accomplishments to preface his new book that is published by Karamat Wilderness Ways.

Today, if a course or instructor has any solid foundation in modern survival skills or Bushcraft, the odds are that they are likely based on a teaching, a skill or idea that Mors had some input in developing – whether they know it or not.

www.ingramcontent.com/pod-product-compliance
Lightning Source LLC
LaVergne TN
LVHW021542080426
835509LV00019B/2785